Gorillas

NorthWord Press
Chanhassen, Minnesota

© NorthWord Press, 2002

Photography © 2002: Anup Shah: cover, pp. 10, 28-29; Ken Lucas/Visuals Unlimited, Inc.: pp. 4, 24-25; Frans Lanting/Minden Pictures: pp. 5, 9, 42-43; Norman Owen Tomalin/Bruce Coleman, Inc.: p. 6; Joe McDonald/Visuals Unlimited, Inc.: p. 13; D. Robert & Lorri Franz: p. 14; Art Wolfe: pp. 16-17, 23; Erwin & Peggy Bauer: p.18; Konrad Wothe/Minden Pictures: pp. 19, 26, 34-35, back cover; Alan Briere: pp. 20-21, 30-31, 44; Kevin Schafer/kevinschafer.com: p. 27; K. & K. Ammann/Bruce Coleman, Inc.: p. 33; Anup Shah/Dembinsky Photo Associates: pp. 38-39; Gerry Ellis/Minden Pictures: p. 41.

Cover image: Male silverback mountain gorilla
Illustrations by John F. McGee
Designed by Russell S. Kuepper
Edited by Judy Gitenstein

NorthWord Press
18705 Lake Drive East
Chanhassen, MN 55317
1-800-328-3895
www.northwordpress.com

Library of Congress Cataloging-in-Publication Data

Dennard, Deborah.
    Gorillas / Deborah Dennard ; illustrations by John McGee.
        p. cm. – (Our wild world series)
    Summary: Discusses the physical characteristics, behavior, habitat, and life cycle of gorillas.
    ISBN 1-55971-844-7 (hardcover) – ISBN 1-55971-843-9 (softcover)
    1. Gorilla—Juvenile literature. [1. Gorilla.] I. McGee, John F., ill. II. Title.
    III. Series.

    QL737.P96 D462 2003
    599.884—dc21   2002032621

Printed in Malaysia

10 9 8 7 6 5 4 3 2 1

Gorillas

Deborah Dennard
Illustrations by John F. McGee

NorthWord Press
Chanhassen, Minnesota

GORILLAS ARE SOME of the most fascinating and misunderstood animals in the world. Gorillas may seem fierce because of their large size, but they are actually very gentle. Gorillas belong to a group of animals called primates (PRY-mates). Humans are primates, too.

All primates have some things in common. Primates have 5 toes on each foot and 5 fingers on each hand. Primates have nails instead of claws on their toes and on their fingers. One of their fingers, the thumb, is special because of the way it moves. This special finger is called an opposable (uh-POE-zih-bull) thumb.

Gorillas are often called gentle giants because of their size, their intelligence, and their largely peaceful nature.

Gorilla mothers are patient with their playful babies and with the curiosity of other youngsters.

Female gorillas and young gorillas, like this one, often climb trees.
Adult males do not because of their size.

Like all primates, gorillas have opposable thumbs
for holding things large and small.

An opposable thumb can move across the palm to touch all of the other fingers. An opposable thumb lets gorillas and other primates hold small things, such as a blade of grass. Primates can also hold larger things, such as rocks.

Opposable thumbs help gorillas groom each other and climb in trees. Opposable thumbs help baby gorillas cling to their mothers. Gorillas and many primates also have opposable big toes. These come in handy for climbing trees. Humans have opposable thumbs, but humans do not have opposable big toes.

Gorillas are found only in parts of central Africa.

There are over 200 kinds, or species (SPEE-sees), in the order of primates. Gorillas, chimpanzees, and orangutans are so much alike they even belong to the same family, the Pongid (PON-djid) family. That family is also called the Great Ape family, so gorillas are a kind of ape.

All apes come from Africa or Asia. All gorillas come from Africa. Gorillas are the largest of all of the apes. Apes are primates, and so are monkeys, but there is a difference. Monkeys have tails, and apes do not.

There are two groups of gorillas: lowland gorillas and mountain gorillas. Lowland gorillas live in the dense, lowland rain forests of central and western Africa.

They have short, brownish-black fur. Mountain gorillas are larger than lowland gorillas. They have long, bluish-black fur. They live high in the cloud forests of the Virunga Mountains in the central African countries of Uganda, Democratic Republic of Congo (Zaire), and Rwanda. Cloud forests are rain forests so high up in the mountains that they are often covered with clouds. They are not tropical, because it is not always hot. It can be quite cool, but it does not freeze.

Gorillas
FUNFACT:

Gorillas are the largest and heaviest primates. They can weigh as much as 400 pounds (180 kilograms). Tiny monkeys, called dwarf bushbabies, are the smallest primates. They weigh just 4 ounces (114 grams)!

Lowland gorillas have short, coarse brownish-black hair.

Mountain gorillas have thick, long hair that is a dark, blue-black color.

There are many differences between male and female gorillas. Male gorillas are larger and heavier than female gorillas. Males may stand 6 feet (1.8 meters) tall and weigh 350 to 400 pounds (160-180 kilograms). Female gorillas may stand 5 feet (1.5 meters) tall and weigh 200 to 250 pounds (90-115 kilograms).

Adult male gorillas that are 15 years or older have long, silver fur on their backs. They are known as silverbacks (SILL-vur-baks). Female gorillas' fur does not turn silver as they get older. Their fur stays black.

Gorillas
FUNFACT:

Scientists take photos of gorilla faces and memorize the nose prints for identification.

The wrinkles around a gorilla's nose are used like fingerprints to help scientists identify individual gorillas. These wrinkles are called nose prints.

Male gorillas have larger canine (KAY-nine) teeth than female gorillas. In male gorillas, powerful muscles reach from the jaw to a ridge of bone on the top of the skull. This ridge of bone makes a crest. Only males have this crest, so their heads are broader and larger than the heads of females. Female gorillas have smaller, rounder heads.

Gorilla arms are longer than their legs. This is true for all apes. Gorillas have large, round, barrel-shaped chests and potbellies. They are not fat, though. Gorillas are made up of hard, strong muscle. They are very powerful animals.

Scientists who study gorillas are able to tell individuals (in-di-VID-ju-uls) apart by what are called nose prints. The wrinkles, folds, and creases that shape gorillas' noses are just as distinctive (dis-TINK-tiv) as human fingerprints. No two gorillas have the same nose print. No two humans have the same fingerprints.

This lowland gorilla uses his large canine teeth to chew tough, fibrous plants as well as for frightening displays.

Gorillas are social animals. Because they are social, they must be able to communicate. Good communication keeps peace in the family group and keeps the family safe from outside danger.

Gorillas have many ways of communicating. They have many ways to show when they are content or when they are excited, angry, or afraid.

Silverback gorillas may become upset when a strange gorilla comes near their family. When this happens, gorillas scream or growl. They thump their chests and shake tree branches. This makes a loud drumming noise that echoes through the forest. Gorillas always use cupped hands for beating their chests. Cupped hands make a much louder noise than closed fists.

As they pound their chests, gorillas roar and growl and grunt. These noisy displays can be heard a mile away in the forest. Younger male gorillas imitate the actions of their leader, and the noise of the group can be extremely loud.

This lowland gorilla is slapping his chest and hooting to show that he is upset.

The stories of gorillas as fierce monsters came from early explorers who watched these displays of strength in gorillas. However, these frightening shows often take the place of actual fights.

When male gorillas do fight, the combat is fierce. They jab and stab and bite with their huge canine teeth.

Gorillas also communicate quietly. They do not look directly at each other. By glancing away and not staring at each other, gorillas show respect and keep the peace. Another form of peaceful communication is grooming. By grooming each other, or picking through each other's fur, gorillas not only keep their fur clean, but reassure each other that all is well.

Gorillas who live in zoos have learned other forms of communication, such as American Sign Language. This demonstrates the high intelligence of these animals.

Gorillas
FUNFACT:

When beating their chests, gorillas may reach a speed of 10 beats per second.

Gorillas are family animals. Most of the time they live in groups of about 12 to 20. Families can be as large as 36 or as small as 5. One silverback male usually leads a family group, which is called a troop. The family may contain several females and their young.

The silverback male is the protector and leader of the gorilla family. He decides when the troop travels, when it stops to feed or rest, and where it spends the night. He will even die protecting his family, if necessary.

Most of the time, life in a gorilla family is peaceful. Young males and females may sometimes quarrel. The silverback male watches from a distance. He only becomes involved if the fighting becomes too noisy or dangerous.

Gorillas
FUNFACT:

The most famous gorilla who knows American Sign Language is Koko. Koko can sign more than 500 words.

Mountain gorillas live in peaceful family troops.

The silver fur on this eastern lowland gorilla's back is a sign that he is a mature adult male.

Within the gorilla family there is an order of strongest to weakest. This is called a pecking order. The silverback leader comes first. He is on top of the pecking order. Other silverbacks come next, then females with babies, and young males whose backs are still black. After that come females without babies. Finally, the youngsters and baby gorillas are at the bottom of the pecking order.

Lower ranking animals show respect to higher ranking ones, often moving out of their way when one wishes to pass. Higher ranking animals get first choice at foods, but all members of the group are well cared for. The silverback leader fathers most of the babies in his troop.

When two strange gorillas meet in the forest, they may scream, pound their chests, or charge at each other.

A silverback male usually guides his family for many years. Gorillas live to be as old as 40, so the members of a gorilla family may spend many years together. When a silverback leader becomes too old or too weak to lead his group, he may be challenged by a younger, stronger silverback. The challenge from the younger gorilla can become noisy and frightening. The two gorillas charge each other, baring their teeth and growling angrily.

The change from one silverback leader to another looks and sounds more violent than it really is, though. In fact, the old leader often stays on as a group member, following the directions of the new silverback leader.

One silverback male is usually the leader of a family, watching over everything they do, and deciding when and where the family eats, travels, rests, and sleeps.

Female gorillas become adults when they are about 8 years old. They leave the family they were born into and search for a new family. All of the gorillas in the new family decide whether to accept the new female. The silverbacks get so excited they beat their chests and shake tree branches. Sometimes silverbacks may fight each other over the arrival of the new female. All of the gorillas hoot and scream as the new female approaches because they do not know yet if she will become one of their family. If the gorilla family accepts the newcomer, she will have a home for the rest of her life. If they do not accept her, she will wander through the forest looking for another family.

Sometimes male gorillas live alone, or a group of young males live together for a few years until they are older. Some lone males and females may even start completely new families.

One of the ways gorillas help each other is by baby-sitting. A mother with an infant may allow another female to take care of her baby during long daily rest periods. The baby-sitting gorilla acts like an aunt or older sister. She grooms and gently plays with the baby and keeps the baby out of trouble.

This baby-sitting behavior is very important. It teaches the baby to accept all members of its family and to be a more social animal. It teaches young females how to take care of babies. This allows them to practice for the day when they will have babies of their own. It also allows the baby's mother to get some rest.

Babies are often at the center of the life of a gorilla family. All members of the gorilla family show interest in new babies. Even males want to touch and sniff newborns.

Gorillas adopt orphaned baby gorillas. Sometimes even a huge silverback will care for an orphaned youngster, sharing his nest and his food and providing safety and comfort to the little one.

Like human babies, gorilla babies take a long time to grow up. They spend a lot of time learning to survive as an adult. It takes about 4 years for a baby gorilla to live without the constant care of its mother.

Gorillas
FUNFACT:

Human babies weigh about 7 pounds (3.2 kilograms) when they are born. Gorilla babies weigh only about 4 pounds (1.8 kilograms) at birth but grow to be as much as 2.5 times the size of humans.

Wild celery is a favorite food of mountain gorillas.
This baby is too young to eat solid food yet.

Most female gorillas are excellent mothers and care for their babies for many years.

Life in the forest is difficult and dangerous. As many as 40 percent of all baby gorillas die in the first 4 years of life. They may get sick or fall while climbing a tree, or they may be illegally hunted by humans.

Adult female gorillas usually have only 1 baby every 7 years. This means it is hard for large numbers of gorillas to be born and grow to adulthood. This is one reason why there are few gorillas left in the world.

It takes a baby about 258 days, nearly 9 months, to grow inside its mother. This is about the same amount of time that a human baby grows inside its mother. Most gorilla babies are born at night in nests made of leaves and sticks. Newborn gorillas have pale pink skin that darkens to black within about a week. They weigh only about 4.5 pounds (2 kilograms) at birth.

When this baby gorilla was an infant, it rode underneath its mother.
Now it is old enough to ride on its mother's back.

Experienced gorilla mothers quickly hold their babies close for warmth and safety and to give their babies milk. First-time mothers may not do as well. Often they do not know how to feed their babies milk. They may not even know how to hold them. New babies from first-time mothers often do not live more than a few days.

Very small babies may be held to the mother's chest for protection. Usually, a newborn baby gorilla holds onto its mother's underside as she moves about in the forest. Each day the baby gorilla's grip grows stronger. As the youngster grows, it climbs on its mother's back.

Baby gorillas stay close to their mothers
but are curious about everything around them.

As young gorillas grow, they begin to move away from their mothers and explore their forest homes.

Baby gorillas grow physically very quickly but need time to learn all it takes to be a gorilla. When they are about 9 or 10 weeks old, they can sit up alone, and they begin to eat solid food. After 4 months, baby gorillas can walk on all fours like adult gorillas. Soon after they can walk, babies begin to play with the other young gorillas in the family.

Young babies often run back to their mothers for comfort. Older babies wrestle and play with each other. This helps them gain strength and coordination (ko-ord-ih-NAY-shun). By playing, they learn the physical skills it takes to be a full-grown gorilla.

Gorilla youngsters may play noisily in pretend battles. They may quietly explore the world around them by touching, smelling, and tasting everything from sticks to flowers to caterpillars. Like human babies, gorilla babies are curious about everything. They learn by experimentation (ex-per-i-men-TAY-shun) and by imitation (imm-i-TAY-shun).

These gorillas pause to rest before moving on to feed some more and find a place for the night.

A gorilla troop's morning begins shortly after dawn when the head silverback wakes everyone. The morning is spent in feeding and finding food. If there is not much food, the troop may travel a long way. If there is a lot of food, they may move very little.

Midday means naptime for the adults and play time for the youngsters. Games are often rough and noisy but are still playful. Sometimes youngsters poke, prod, and pull on their elders who are trying to sleep. This does not bother adult gorillas. Usually they just ignore the youngsters and pretend to sleep.

During the rest period gorillas clean and groom their own fur. Mothers make sure their babies are well-groomed. Mothers use their fingers and fingernails to comb through their babies' hair. They lick or gently nibble out any dirt or insects in the hair. They touch and pat and cuddle their babies. Gorillas often make low coughing noises during grooming. It is signal that everything is okay.

Gorillas
FUNFACT:

Gorillas are so large that a footprint left behind may measure as long as 12 inches (30.5 centimeters).

This gorilla is using his opposable thumb to eat some wild celery.

Fields of crops are planted so close to the gorillas' forests that gorillas are sometimes seen in a field such as this one. Farmers may consider gorillas to be threats to their crops.

After the midday rest time, gorillas usually travel and eat until early evening.

A gorilla troop's territory each day is not very large, but over a year gorillas may travel far in search of food. Because of the dense forest in which gorillas live, it is difficult for scientists to know much about gorilla territories. Some studies show gorilla territories are only about 1.5 square miles (about 4 square kilometers). Other studies show their territories to be much larger. There is still a lot to learn about gorillas.

In the evenings, the gorilla troop finds a place to stop for the night. Then they gather plants and sticks that they will use to make nests. This is where the gorillas will sleep.

A gorilla's nest is a circle of plants and sticks pulled toward the center,
making a comfortable circle. Smaller gorillas make nests in trees.
Larger gorillas make nests on the ground.

Gorillas build their nests on the ground or in the lower branches of a tree. The nests are usually not far from the troop's last feeding stop of the day.

A gorilla's nest is a circle of plants and sticks about 6 to 8 feet (1.8 to 2.4 meters) around. Gorillas can build their nests very quickly, in just a matter of minutes.

The lead silverback is the first to begin building his nest. The others in his troop pick spots around him, often according to age and pecking order in the troop.

Babies under 2.5 years old sleep with their mothers. All other gorillas sleep alone.

Gorillas
FUNFACT:

Scientists study the sleeping nests left behind by gorillas. They can guess the number of gorillas in a family and even the ages of each of the family members.

His forest home provides this gorilla with shelter,
safety, and all the food he can find.

Gorillas live on a diet of leaves and fruits. They crush their food with their large, flat molar (MOH-ler) teeth. Gorillas eat many types of plants. They eat ferns, shrubs, grasses, vines, trees, and leafy plants.

Gorillas eat just about every part of these plants. They eat the fruits, stems, flowers, shoots, bulbs, leaves, and bark. Gorillas use their opposable thumbs and flexible fingers to gather food.

Gorillas
FUNFACT:

Gorillas do not usually drink water in the wild. Most of the water they need comes from the plants they eat.

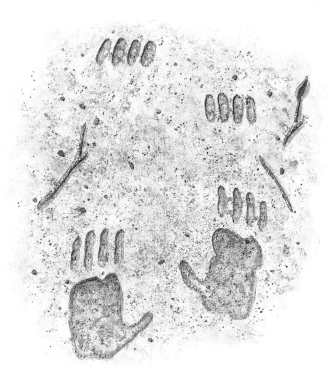

**Gorilla tracks show that they walk flat-footed.
They curl their hands into fists to walk on their knuckles.**

Gorillas walk using their arms and legs. They curl their hands into fists and lean on their knuckles with each step. This is called knuckle walking. Their feet are placed flat on the ground when they walk.

Gorillas spend most of their time on the ground. When they see tasty fruit and leaves in the trees, gorillas can climb up to get them. They use their hands and feet and climb slowly but confidently up the tree. They can climb as high as 100 feet (30.5 meters) above the ground in search of food.

When climbing down from trees, gorillas move slowly and carefully. They go down with their feet first. Whether they are on the ground or in the trees, gorillas are most comfortable when moving with all 4 limbs. Smaller females and young gorillas regularly explore trees. Adult male gorillas climb in the trees less often and with greater caution because of their heavy weight.

Baby gorillas learn to climb and soon become
independent from their mothers.

Gorillas of every age live together in a troop.
Sometimes older sisters help care for younger siblings.

There are very few gorillas left in the world today. Gorillas are an endangered (en-DANE-jurd) species. Mountain gorillas are even more rare than lowland gorillas.

Sometimes humans hunt gorillas for food or for pets. This is illegal. Without protection (pro-TEK-shun) from people, they may become extinct (ex-TINKD). This means they may die out completely.

Gorillas are losing their forest homes. As the human population of Africa grows, more and more land is needed for growing crops, for raising cattle, and for people to live. To make more land for people, land is taken away from gorillas.

Even mountain gorilla babies have thick, long hair.

In 1999 scientists counted about 100,000 lowland gorillas. This is not a large number compared to the number of gorillas there used to be. Most of these gorillas are found in the tiny country of Gabon, in Africa. Gabon has very few people and is mostly filled with forests that are perfect for gorillas. As long as the forests are safe, gorillas are safe.

Scientists counted only about 600 mountain gorillas in 1999. Uganda, Democratic Republic of Congo (Zaire), and Rwanda, where mountain gorillas live, have many, many people. Every year more forest is lost, and more gorillas are lost.

The people in these crowded countries often go to war with each other. When the people fight, gorillas are often killed as well.

Gorillas are some of the most popular animals found in zoos today. While gorillas thrive best in the wild, zoo gorillas are important to the survival of all gorillas. They help teach scientists about gorilla behavior.

Once considered ferocious, gorillas are now often called the gentle giants of the jungle. If their forest homes can be saved, then gorillas can be saved. As long as there is rain forest that is safe from people, there will be gorillas in the world, and the gentle giants will live on.

Internet Sites

You can find out more interesting information about gorillas and lots of other wildlife by visiting these Internet sites.

www.congogorillaforest.com/	Bronx Zoo
www.enchantedlearning.com	Enchanted Learning.com
www.fonz.org	Friends of the National Zoo
www.kidsplanet.org	Defenders of Wildlife
www.koko.org/kidsclub	Koko's Kids Club
www.nationalgeographic.com/kids/creature_feature/0007/gorillas.html	
	National Geographic.com
www.pbs.org/wnet/nature/koko/	PBS Online
www.primate.org	Primate Conservation, Inc.
ww2.zoo.nsw.gov.au/zoo.net/gorilla/index.aspx	Taronga Zoo
http://wcs.org/7823	Wildlife Conservation Society

Index

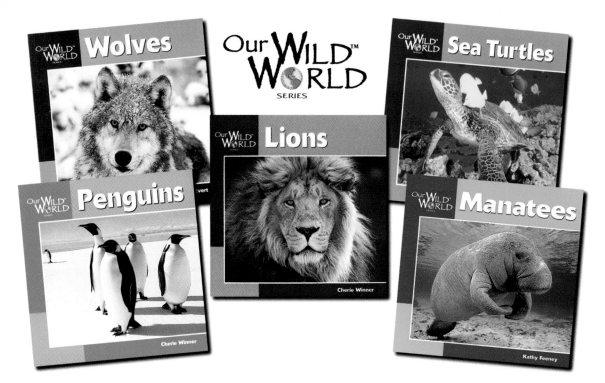

Titles available in the Our Wild World Series:

See your nearest bookseller, or order by phone 1-800-328-3895

NORTHWORD PRESS
Chanhassen, Minnesota